RICHARD THE LIONHEART AND THE CRUSADES

Christopher Gibb

Illustrations by Gerry Wood

The Bookwright Press
New York · 1985

LIFE AND TIMES

Julius Caesar and the Romans
Alfred the Great and the Saxons
Canute and the Vikings
William the Conqueror and the Normans
Richard the Lionheart and the Crusades
Columbus and the Age of Exploration
Elizabeth I and Tudor England

Further titles are in preparation

First published in the United States in 1985 by
The Bookwright Press
387 Park Avenue South
New York, NY 10016

First published in 1985 by
Wayland (Publishers) Ltd
49 Lansdowne Place, Hove
East Sussex BN3 1HF, England

ISBN 0-531-18011 5
Library of Congress Catalog Card Number 84-73571

Printed in Italy by G. Canale & C.S.p.A., Turin

Contents

1 THE STORY OF RICHARD

The legend

Below *Richard's small force of crusaders defending the walls of Jaffa against the attacking Saracens.*

On a scorching August morning in 1192, King Richard's tiny crusading army faced defeat. Drawn up before the wall of Jaffa, in the Holy Land, were rank upon rank of Saracen warriors under their formidable leader, Saladin. Throughout that long, hot morning Richard's small band of 54 knights and 15 horses beat off repeated charges by Saladin's cavalry. In mid-afternoon, Richard led his exhausted knights on an attack. Saladin, watching from his

tent, was overcome with admiration for his courageous enemy. When he saw Richard fall as his horse was killed under him, he sent a servant leading two fresh horses as a present from one king to another.

Many legends surround the life of Richard I, King of England from 1189 to 1199. Enormously tall and strikingly handsome, he was undoubtedly the most famous warrior of his time. It was his exploits on the battlefield that earned him the nickname Coeur-de-Lion — the "Lionheart." What is less well-known is that he was also an amateur poet and musician and an accomplished scholar.

But there was a darker side to Richard's character. Much of his early life was spent in fighting against his father and brothers. He could also be extremely cruel, punishing rebellions in his French lands with savage ferocity. Despite all this, his soldiers adored him.

In 1187, an event occurred that was to change Richard's life. In that year the Christian knights who were defending the Holy Land were defeated by Saladin, and Jerusalem was captured by the Saracens. From that moment, Richard's one desire was to lead an army to recapture the Holy City.

Above *The statue of Richard the Lionheart outside the Houses of Parliament in London.*

The crusader

Above *Richard the Lionheart watches the execution of Saracen hostages after the siege of Acre in 1191.*

Richard was crowned King of England on September 3, 1189. He at once set about raising an army for the Holy Land. He believed so passionately in this cause, that he declared he would sell London to pay for the crusades if only he could find a buyer!

The journey to the Holy Land of Palestine was a long and adventurous one. It took Richard over a year to reach his destination. On the way he managed to rescue his sister Joan from the hands of the King of Sicily, get married and capture the island of Cyprus. At last, on July 8, 1191, Richard joined the crusader army camped before the heavily fortified town of Acre.

For two long years the crusaders had been battering the walls of Acre, a coastal fortress they needed to capture to reach Jerusalem. Disease raged in the Christian camp and most newcomers fell sick as soon as they arrived. Richard was no exception. The story goes that Saladin sent fresh fruit to Richard's tent to aid his recovery. Richard replied with a gift of falcons. It is incidents such as these that

make the story of Richard so romantic.

Acre eventually surrendered to the crusaders. When Saladin failed to release his Christian captives, Richard had all his prisoners executed in sight of the Saracen army. He also quarreled with his allies, King Philip of France and Duke Leopold of Austria. Both men took their armies home in disgust.

Richard himself stayed over a year in the Holy Land. Twice he defeated the mighty Saladin, first at the battle of Arsuf and then at Jaffa, but he was unable to capture Jerusalem. On two occasions he led his army within sight of its walls, but Richard refused to gaze on the distant Holy City which God would not let him deliver.

Below *Richard leads the crusading army as it marches down the coast of the Holy Land.*

7

Capture and death

When peace was eventually made with Saladin in 1192, Richard was eager to return home to England. Disturbing rumors had reached him that his brother John was plotting to overthrow him. But Richard's adventures were far from over. On his way back across Europe he was captured by the duke of Austria — the very man whom he had insulted at Acre by having his banner trampled in the mud. He was shut up in an impregnable fortress overlooking the Danube River.

Legend has it that Richard's faithful companion Blondel searched for his master across Europe, singing songs of their homeland until he heard an answering song from a barred window. The story may or may not be true.

Below *Returning to England after the Crusade, Richard was imprisoned in a fortress on the Danube River by the duke of Austria. He was discovered there by his faithful companion, Blondel.*

It is certainly the sort of romantic tale Richard would have enjoyed.

Richard was ransomed for 150,000 marks — a huge sum, even today. All the ransom money was raised by his English subjects, despite opposition from Prince John who would have preferred to let his famous brother rot in prison. The fact that the money was raised shows how popular Richard was, and also how prosperous England had become by the end of the twelfth century. Such was his fearsome reputation that when Richard finally landed in England, a party of rebels immediately surrendered, their leader having died of fright when he heard of the king's return!

Richard did not spend long in England. Indeed he stayed barely six months in his kingdom during the ten years of his reign. The last years of his life were spent quarreling over his French lands with his rival, King Philip of France. Although he always meant to return to the Holy Land with a fresh army, he never did. He met his death from an arrow wound received while besieging a small castle in southwest France. He was only forty-one.

Above *The Great Seal of King Richard.*

The Great Seal of Richard's brother, John, was used to give authority to his decisions when he was King of England from 1199 to 1216.

2 BACKGROUND TO THE CRUSADES

The Holy Places

Jesus Christ was born in Bethlehem and crucified in Jerusalem: these two towns in Palestine are the most sacred shrines in the Christian religion. The Emperor Constantine recognized Christianity as the official religion of his Roman Empire in A.D. 325. His mother, St. Helena, journeyed to Jerusalem. There she built the Church of the Holy Sepulcher over the spot where Christ had been crucified. Another great church was built at Bethlehem. Pilgrims came from all over the Roman Empire to visit these Holy Places.

Constantine also founded a new capital at Byzantium, renamed Constantinople in his honor. From that time on the Roman Empire was divided between an empire of the west, based at Rome, and an eastern empire at Constantinople, usually called the Byzantine Empire. The western empire did not last long. In the fifth century A.D. it was overrun by warlike barbarians. Much of Roman civilization was destroyed and northwest Europe fell into the gloom of the Dark Ages.

In the east, however, the Byzantine Empire flourished. By the year 600, the emperor at Constantinople was by far the most powerful ruler in the known world. His subjects were devout Christians, but the organization of the eastern Church was very different from that of the Roman Church. In the east, the emperor was the unquestioned head of the Church; in the west all Christians obeyed the pope in Rome. This division of the Christian churches was to cause many bitter quarrels during the Crusades. However, a new religion had arisen in the east that was to threaten Christians everywhere and change the history of Europe.

Above *A fifteenth century painting showing pilgrims approaching the walled city of Jerusalem.*

Opposite *Constantinople, the capital of the Byzantine Empire, was a rich and flourishing city before the Crusades.*

11

Islam

Above *The Prophet Mohammed prays to the Muslim god, Allah, in the wilderness.*

In A.D. 622, a young Arab called Mohammed began to preach to his countrymen in Arabia. Mohammed spent much of his early life accompanying the great camel caravans that crisscrossed the bleak wilderness that made up so much of the interior of his country. It was in the desert that his thoughts turned to God.

Mohammed was a simple man, with simple ideas about worship. He rejected the complicated ideas of Christianity. Instead he believed in one virtuous God who rewarded believers and punished sinners. He admitted that there had been prophets before, among whom Jesus Christ was one, but he was convinced that he himself had been chosen to complete God's teachings. This new religion was called "Islam" and its followers were known as "True Believers" or "Muslims." Christians feared and despised them, calling them "Infidels."

Ten years after Mohammed's death, Islam was supreme in Arabia. The Arabs now set out to conquer the world for the new faith. They met with amazing success. In 638 Jerusalem fell to their armies. But the Christian Church within the Holy City still survived. Mohammed had laid down strict rules about how conquered people who would not accept Islam should be treated. For those who believed in many gods there was no mercy, but Christians and Jews were allowed to live in peace under their Muslim masters because they believed in only one God.

So pilgrims from all over Christendom continued to visit the Holy Places. By 1050, pilgrims were visiting Jerusalem in large numbers. A new migration of fierce eastern tribesmen was to change all this.

Above *Arab soldiers set out to conquer the world for Islam.*

Below *The map shows the division of the known world into areas controlled by either Christians or Muslims.*

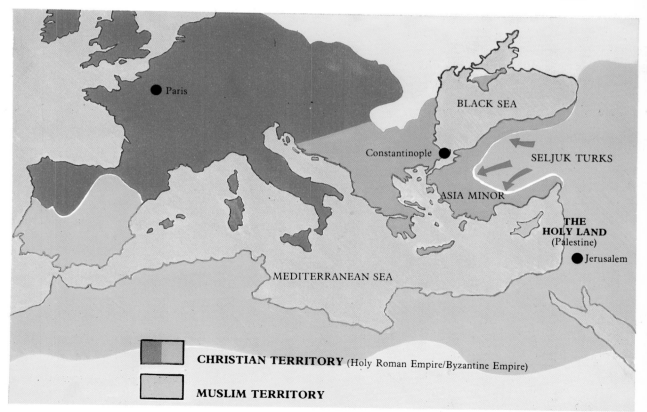

CHRISTIAN TERRITORY (Holy Roman Empire/Byzantine Empire)

MUSLIM TERRITORY

The Seljuk Turks

Above *During the eleventh century, the Byzantine Empire was under constant attack from bands of warlike Seljuk Turks.*

In the middle years of the eleventh century, fierce bands of wandering Turks appeared on the edge of the Byzantine Empire. They were impressed by Arab civilization and became Muslims — but they were as yet untamed by Islam.

As the years went by, Turkish raids into Christian territory became more and more frequent. In 1071 the Emperor Romanus Diogenes met the Turks in the great battle of Manzikert on his eastern frontier. He was heavily defeated. Turkish bands now roamed freely through Asia Minor (present-day Turkey), destroying settlements and killing peasants. Soon one of the most civilized parts of the Byzantine Empire was little more than a desert.

Syria and Palestine were also in chaos. Every city was governed by a rival Turkish or Arab chieftain, constantly at war with the other. It was now unsafe for pilgrims to make the journey to the Holy Land from the west.

In 1095, the Emperor Alexius appealed to the pope for help. He had heard of the skill of western knights and hoped to recruit some for his army. Appeals of this sort had reached the west before, but the pope usually chose to ignore them. This time Pope Urban II did not. He had his own reasons for falling in with Alexius's request. He saw much of western Europe devastated by famine and civil war. He saw knights using their superior power to rob their neighbors and kill the poor. Here was a chance to unite all Christians in a Holy War. Urban may also have thought that if his expedition was successful, he could rightfully claim to be the overall Christian leader of both east and west.

Alexius Comnenus I, Byzantine Emperor from 1081 to 1118.

15

Preaching the Crusade

Above *Pope Urban II, who launched the First Crusade with his fiery sermons.*

On a cold November day in 1095, a jostling crowd of knights, merchants, pilgrims and peasants gathered in the market place of Clermont in France. The crowd parted as a small, gaunt figure made his way to a simple wooden platform. The pope had come to speak to his people.

Raising his voice above the chill wind, Urban II spoke of the wickedness of the west and the dangers threatening the Christians in the east. Turning to the assembled lords and knights he cried, "You, the oppressors of children, plunderers of widows and robbers of others' rights . . . if you wish to be mindful of your souls, advance boldly as knights of Christ to the defense of the eastern Church."

The pope went on to tell of the suffering of the Church in Jerusalem. He exhorted the crowd to "drive out the Turks who are in this land, and may you deem it a beautiful thing to die for Christ in that city in which he died for us." This was what really appealed to the crowd. Thousands volunteered at once, and the meeting broke up in confusion. Few realized that Urban had cleverly changed the emperor's appeal to suit his own wishes. His knights of Christ were not asked to help the emperor's army, but to free the Holy Places from the infidels.

Right *In 1095 Pope Urban II preached the Crusade to a large crowd in Clermont in France.*

Details of the expedition were soon worked out by the pope and his bishops. All volunteers would wear a red cross sewn on to their white tunics. In Latin they were called "crucesignati," and this is where we get the word "crusader." All who fought would be pardoned their sins. Nine months later, the expedition gathered in Constantinople.

The Emperor Alexius's call for help had been answered, but he was going to get more than he bargained for . . .

3 THE TWO SIDES

Romance and reality

Songs, heroic poems and ballads voiced over the centuries, portray the Crusades as a romantic struggle by brave knights who gave up everything to fight Christ's battles. Albert of Aix, a knight-poet of the First Crusade, gives us a highly colorful picture of the Christian army: "The crusaders in all the splendor of their shields of gold, green, red and other colors, unfurling banners of gold and purple, marched towards Antioch, mounted on

great horses." The Saracens, on the other hand, were condemned as cruel, evil and vicious.

There is no doubt that the Saracens could be cruel. They delighted in torturing their captives, and some had the skulls of their enemies mounted in silver as trophies. But the crusaders were just as cruel and often committed worse crimes. At the siege of Antioch during the First Crusade, the Norman leader, Bohemond, had his captives killed and roasted as if for a cannibal feast.

Many knights became crusaders more with the idea of plunder and riches than for any deep religious reasons. Both sides were guilty of massacring their opponents when they fell into their hands. But few slaughters can compare with the capture of Jerusalem during the First Crusade in 1099. As a contemporary wrote: "There was such a carnage that our men were wading in Saracen blood up to their ankles."

Not all crusaders were so bloodthirsty. Many sincerely believed in their cause and acted with mercy and generosity to their enemies. But perhaps the most chivalrous warrior of all was Saladin, the great Saracen leader. There was no massacre when he recaptured Jerusalem from the crusaders in 1187.

Above *A well armed Saracen warrior brandishes his scimitar.*

Lords and knights

As we have seen, Pope Urban II had little respect for knights. He saw clearly that most of them lived for war and little else. The Crusades were partially an attempt to get them to behave better: to fight for God and not their own greed.

The barbarians who overran the western Roman Empire were the first to prove how invincible heavily armed horsemen could be. By the eleventh century, cavalry was supreme, as William the Conqueror proved at the Battle of Hastings in 1066. But to equip yourself as a knight was an expensive business which few could afford.

Above and below *A knight kneels before his lord and swears an oath of loyalty to him.*

It was because of this, and also because the times were so lawless that men felt they needed another's protection, that a system developed in northwest Europe called feudalism.

Feudal comes from the word "faith," because a knight was supposed to make an oath of faith to his lord — the person one step higher on the feudal ladder. In return, the knight would be given a piece of land from which he could raise money to pay for his knightly equipment. This oath of faith bound a man to fight for his lord in time of war. The great lords — the dukes and counts — would in their turn make an oath to the king in return for their land. The king stood at the top of the feudal pyramid — though the pope constantly claimed he was above everyone else. What was not in doubt was that the poor peasants were at the base, and were often treated little better than slaves.

The organization of medieval society was based on the knight. The knight was primarily a warrior, so western Europe spent most of its time at war. Lords and knights were constantly fighting one another and robbing the poor. The romantic tales of King Arthur's "noble knights" are mostly mythical.

Above *A crusading knight kneels and prays before going into battle.*

Below *This fourteenth century painting shows knights getting ready to sail for the Holy Land on a Crusade.*

The ordinary soldiers

Below *Bear-baiting was one of the few entertainments enjoyed by the peasants whose lives otherwise were dull and hard.*

Too concerned with romantic tales of knights and battles, history has often overlooked the fate of the peasants who formed the bulk of the people. Crusading armies were filled with these peasants who had to endure terrible suffering.

In the same way that a knight "borrowed" his land from his lord, so a peasant was given a small strip of land to cultivate on the estate of a knight. In return he became virtually a slave. He had to plant and harvest his lord's crops as well as his own. He could not leave his village without his lord's permission and he even had to hand over a fifth of his meager crop to his master.

Many lords behaved brutally towards their peasants. It was almost impossible for a humble peasant to appeal against such treatment, as the courts were usually run by the lord himself. Life was a weary round of drudgery and hunger, with famines sweeping the countryside about once every ten years. There was almost no entertainment, except for the occasional bear-baiting or wandering juggler. Education was nonexistent.

It is no wonder that so many of the poor jumped at the chance of leaving their miserable existence for the adventures of a Crusade. Religion was often the most important part of their lives, and they believed more passionately in the crusading cause than many of the knights and lords. The pope had appealed for recruits from all Christians, so if a lord attempted to prevent a peasant from going, he was challenging not only the wishes of the pope but also the wishes of God. So thousands set out to become footsoldiers in the crusading armies. Very few were to return.

Left *Peasants harvest the crops for their lord of the manor (from a twelfth century manuscript).*

The Saracens

It often suited a knight to see his enemy as a treacherous, cruel barbarian. But in many ways, Arab civilization in the twelfth century was more advanced than that of the countries that today make up western Europe.

Pilgrims and crusaders alike were impressed by the well-watered fields of northern Syria, with their neat villages full of orchards and beautiful gardens. They might gape too, at the bustling bazaars of Tripoli or Antioch. A chronicler records the amazement of two knights on a visit to Cairo in Egypt, "We saw fountains of marble filled with sparkling water, over which flocks of birds unknown to us fluttered and sang. Galleries were lined with marble columns, sheathed with gold and covered with carvings."

In the pursuit of learning, the Muslim scholar far outstripped his Christian rival. Science, astronomy and medicine were much more advanced in the east. Indeed a wise crusader would employ an Arab doctor to tend his wounds, rather than one of his own countrymen.

The more thoughtful crusader recognized the fine qualities of his opponent. Even the official account of the First Crusade praises the Saracens: "In truth, had they but kept the faith of Christ, none could have equaled them in power, courage and the arts of war."

Below *This twelfth century illustration shows two Muslim doctors discussing their patient's illness. At that time, the Arabs knew far more about medicine than their Christian rivals.*

Right *Crusaders thought that all Saracens were barbarians, but in fact many Arabs lived in great splendor and were more civilized than their Christian enemies.*

4 THE FIRST CRUSADE

The People's Crusade

Below *In 1096 Peter the Hermit led a bedraggled column of crusaders to disaster at the hands of the Turks in Asia Minor.*

The response to Pope Urban's appeal for a Crusade was astonishing. All over Europe men, women and children swarmed to take the Cross. "God wills it," the priests cried, and the poor were only too willing to believe them.

One preacher in particular caused a sensation. Peter the Hermit had recently tried to visit Jerusalem and had been badly treated by the Saracens. Half-naked, with mad, staring eyes, he whipped his audiences into a state of religious hysteria. He soon had an army of followers. Led by Peter and a few disreputable knights, the rabble set off for

Left *Constantinople, the center of the Byzantine Empire (from the Nuremburg Chronicles).*

Constantinople. Lacking money and supplies, they were led more by dreams than by good sense.

The high religious ideals of the crusaders were soon stained with blood. Marching through Germany, they massacred thousands of Jews. In eastern Europe they pillaged the countryside in search of food and were themselves attacked by the local inhabitants. Only a third of the original force reached Constantinople.

The Emperor Alexius was taken by surprise. This was not the sort of army he had expected. When the crusaders began to rob and burn in Constantinople itself, he quickly hustled them across the Bosporus Strait to Asia Minor.

This poor, ill-fed army of peasants, so ignorantly marching to a Holy War, was no match for the fierce Turks. In a series of ambushes and sieges, all were massacred or enslaved. There was left such a pile of bones at the fortress of Civetot, it was written at the time, that later crusaders used them to repair the walls, "and thus made of that city as it were their tomb."

The great lords ride out

From France, Normandy and southern Italy, the lords and knights were preparing to set out, some traveling as part of the army of a powerful lord while others traveled singly, with perhaps a couple of servants.

By the spring of 1097 most of the army had reached Constantinople. Almost at once, disagreements arose between the Byzantines and the crusaders. The crusaders wanted to press on to the Holy Land and were not interested in helping the emperor. Alexius himself had no intention of joining in a Holy War. He gave the crusaders money and shipped them across to Asia Minor.

Striking out across Asia Minor, the crusading army had its first great battle with the Turks at Dorylaeum. It was a very close thing. The army had been marching in two

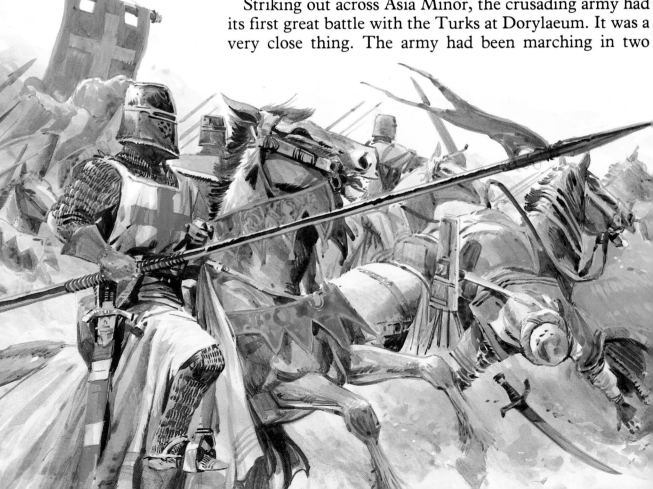

columns, the first commanded by Bohemond, a Norman brigand but a magnificent soldier, and the second by Raymond, Count of Toulouse. These two leaders were great rivals. As Bohemond struck camp on July 1, 1097, he was attacked by a large army of Turks. After six hours of fierce fighting the crusaders began to waver. In the nick of time, Raymond arrived with the heavy cavalry of the second column, having galloped a day's journey in a couple of hours. A third force under the warlike Bishop Adhemar rode around to take the Turks in the rear. The infidel army broke up in panic.

Elated by their success, the crusaders resumed their march to Palestine. Now heat, lack of water and disease became the main enemy. More crusaders died in the deserts of Asia Minor and the mountains of northern Syria than at Dorylaeum. It was a much depleted army that eventually arrived to besiege the great Muslim fortress of Antioch.

Above *An engraving of crusaders fighting the Turks at Constantinople in 1097.*

Left *In 1097 the crusading army routed the Turks at the battle of Dorylaeum.*

Jerusalem recaptured

Below Trapped inside Antioch by the Saracens, the crusaders uncovered a lance-head. A priest claimed that it was the one that speared Jesus Christ's side on the Cross.

The crusaders spent nearly a year before the walls of Antioch. Conditions in the besieged city and the Christian camp were appalling. Both sides were reduced to eating rats and lizards.

Antioch finally fell to the Christians through the treachery of a Muslim leader. They only just entered the fortress in time. Three days later a huge Saracen army appeared before the city. The crusaders were trapped inside Antioch in their turn.

It was at this moment that a strange event occurred. A humble priest, Peter Batholomew, claimed a vision had shown him where the spear that had pierced Christ's side on the Cross was buried. Feverishly the crusaders set about digging, and unearthed an old iron lance-head.

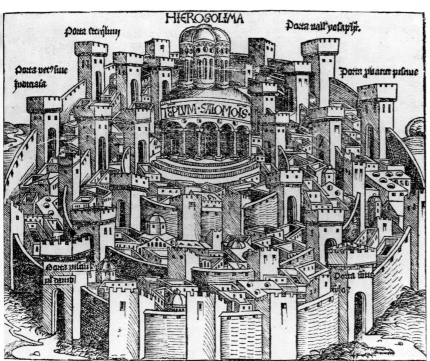

Along the top of the drawing: **HIEROSOLIMA**

Porta ccnlinii · Porta vall'yofaphr · Porta vct'fuie judaica · Porta pharic pifane · TEPLVM·SALOMOIS · Porta pilati pl dauid · Porta fctti hioz

Greatly inspired by this discovery, the Christian army marched out of Antioch with the "Holy Lance" at their head, and defeated the huge Saracen army. The way to Jerusalem now lay open.

Religious hysteria possessed many crusaders as they approached the Holy City. Individual knights galloped on ahead just for a glimpse of its walls. It was hot and excessively dry as the army encamped before Jerusalem. The crusaders knew they would have to fight their way in quickly or die of thirst. Siege towers and battering rams were built, and the whole army walked barefoot around the city, fasting and praying. Then the assault began. After a hectic day of fighting the first knights gained a foothold on the walls. "As soon as they reached the top," recorded an eyewitness, "all the defenders of the town fled through the city and our men followed them and harried them, felling and killing them."

After a day of slaughter, Jerusalem had been won back for Christ, but in Christ's name the crusaders had captured a city of stinking corpses.

Above *Crusaders, besieged in Antioch, are cheered by the miraculous discovery of the "Holy Lance."*

5 CONDITIONS ON CRUSADE

Rival armies

The chief strength of the crusading army lay in its knights. The knight wore a long mailshirt of iron links, reaching from his shoulders to his calves. On his head sat a conical steel cap with a vertical bar to protect his face. By King Richard's time a larger helmet was used which covered the entire head. But you couldn't wear it for long in the Holy Land or you were likely to cook! The knight was armed with a lance used in the charge, a heavy

Below *The heavily armed knight on horseback was the finest soldier in the crusading army.*

double-edged sword for closer combat and a kite-shaped shield. To carry his great weight, a knight rode an expensive warhorse.

No soldiers in the world could withstand charging knights, but the charge had its limitations. If an enemy gave ground before a knight, the horse was soon exhausted. Moreover, knights were not used to fighting in large numbers, or obeying orders from a single leader.

The main strength of the Saracen armies was also in their horsemen, but these were very different from the heavily armed knights. Their main weapon was the bow. Mounted on lighter, faster horses than the crusaders, the Saracens would gallop in front of the enemy line shooting their arrows — often deliberately aiming at the warhorses. They would then all charge together, unsheathing their razor-sharp scimitars for use at close quarters.

Below *The lightly armed Saracens rode smaller and more maneuverable horses. They always tried to avoid pitched battles, which were better suited to the tactics of the crusading knights.*

Sieges and castles

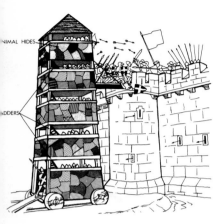

Above *The crusaders used massive siege towers, similar to this one, to force their way into Jerusalem in 1099.*

Every knight was used to besieging castles of the wooden, motte-and-bailey type. But the crusaders were amazed by the fortresses they saw in the east. When confronted with the massive stone walls of Antioch, the crusaders could not imagine how they would ever get inside them.

An attacking army had several alternatives when confronted by a strong castle. The besiegers could try to starve the garrison into surrendering or bribe their way in, as Bohemond did at Antioch. If this also failed, the attackers would have to attempt an assault.

Huge siege "engines" were built by the crusaders at Jerusalem. The most effective were tall, wooden siege towers which could be dragged to the walls. Wet hide was stretched across their exposed timbers to protect them from the fearsome "Greek fire" — a mixture of oil and tar which could be ignited and sprayed on besieging troops as they clambered up the castle walls. A "flying" bridge was attached to the top to allow the attackers to gain a foothold on the walls. Machines like giant sling shots, or catapults, were also used to fling huge stones at weak points in the defenses.

The crusaders were quick to learn from the castles in the east. They copied them when building their own frontier fortresses in the Holy Land. Krak des Chevaliers, in Syria, is a magnificent example of a crusader castle. They also brought these new ideas back to Europe with them. Richard I used all the latest techniques from the east when he built his fortress at Chateau Gaillard in northern France and strengthened the Tower of London.

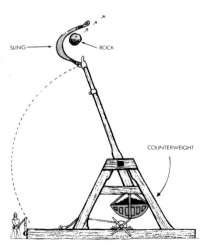

Left *This trebuchet was used to hurl huge stones over the city walls.*

Above *"Greek Fire" pours from the battlements of a fort the crusaders are besieging.*

Left *A common siege weapon was the mangonel which worked like an enormous catapult.*

Life on the road

Above *Tragedy often befell the crusaders as they marched over treacherous mountain passes on their way to the Holy Land.*

There were two main routes to the Holy Land from western Europe, and both were hazardous. The pilgrim or knight could travel south and take a ship from the toe of Italy but the terrifying experience of men and horses tumbling about in a stinking hold as their ship was lashed by storms discouraged many a would-be crusader.

Most early crusading armies chose to travel overland via Constantinople and Asia Minor. This route was so dangerous that hundreds of thousands were to die without ever reaching the Holy Land. Once over the Bosporus, Turkish horsemen would harry the Christian armies right across Asia Minor. The ordinary pilgrims — old men, women and children — were especially vulnerable to such attacks. As the crusaders marched eastwards they would find the wells dry, the grass burned and the fields

uncultivated. Heat, exhaustion and thirst took a heavy toll. An added danger came from flash storms. As a chronicler wrote, "I saw many of our people perish from these cold rains, for lack of tents to shelter in."

Having crossed the deserts, the weary Christians then had to face the mountains. An eyewitness wrote, "The horses fell headlong into ravines, one pack animal dragging down another. On every side the knights gave way to despair." More died here than in the deserts.

Asia Minor was the graveyard of many brave expeditions. In 1190, the German Emperor Barbarossa marched on the Third Crusade with a huge army of 300,000. His knights easily beat the Turks in every encounter, but sickness, hunger and thirst turned horses and men into skeletons. Barbarossa himself was accidentally drowned on the journey. Disheartened and leaderless, only 2,000 of his army eventually joined the other crusaders at Acre.

Barbarossa, the German emperor from 1155 to 1190.

Life in the Holy Land

Once Jerusalem was captured in 1099, a great number of crusaders went home, their task done. But others decided to stay in the Holy Land. Many of these men were younger sons with no land in Europe, and they were eager to carve out rich estates for themselves in Palestine. Some of the great lords also stayed. They elected one of their number, Godfrey of Bouillon, to become their leader. Within a year of Godfrey's death, his brother Baldwin became the first King of Jerusalem. Other crusading states were also established: the three main ones were Edessa, Antioch and Tripoli.

In the century that followed, a division arose between those crusaders who were simply making a short pilgrimage to Jerusalem, and those who were there to stay. These

Below *Crusading knights, newly arrived in the Holy Land, were disgusted to see some well-established crusaders dressing and acting like Saracens.*

permanent settlers, or "barons of the land," began by building castles to protect their lands and fought continuously with their neighbors.

But the crusaders who stayed behind soon realized that they could not fight the Saracens all the time. They had to make truces with their Muslim neighbors to protect their own lands. Some began to wear turbans and long silk gowns because they were cooler in the hot climate. Others built tinkling fountains in the courtyards of their castles. A few even learned Arabic.

The noble pilgrims who had journeyed to the Holy Land to pray at the Holy Places and kill a few Saracens, couldn't understand this at all. Hadn't the pope told them that it was their holy duty to kill all Saracens? Word began to reach Europe that the "barons of the land" were becoming infidels themselves. When the Saracen forces became stronger in the second half of the twelfth century, this division between the crusaders was to prove fatal.

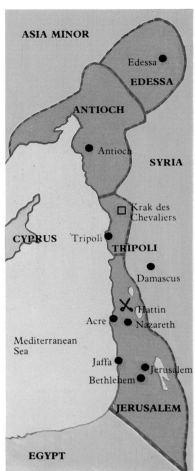

Above *The map shows the four crusader states of Edessa, Antioch, Tripoli and Jerusalem, at the start of the twelfth century.*

Assassins and fighting monks

Above *The "Old Man of the Mountain" shows a drugged man a glimpse of Paradise before recruiting him for the Assassins — a group of professional killers.*

One of the strangest and most terrifying groups that the crusaders encountered in the east was the Muslim sect of Assassins. This secret group of fanatics was founded by a Persian known as the "Old Man of the Mountain."

In his mountain fortress in Persia, he laid out a beautiful garden, peopled with lovely girls and stocked with delicious food. A follower would be drugged, taken to the garden, and allowed to sample its delights. Afterwards, he would be told that he had just visited Paradise, and if he died serving the Old Man, he would return there forever. The Old Man would then use him to assassinate one of his enemies, knowing his follower would do it without fear of death. The Old Man's successors hired assassins to murder anyone, Christian or Muslim, and paid them handsomely.

The fiercest and most dedicated soldiers on the Christian side were two orders of fighting monks called

the Knights of St. John (or the Hospitalers), and the Knights Templar. The Knights of St. John were originally ordinary monks who ran a hospital in Jerusalem for Christian pilgrims. But they soon became an independent military force, guarding pilgrims as they crossed the Holy Land. The Templars were founded to guard the Holy Places and had their headquarters in the Temple of Solomon in Jerusalem.

These knights were to provide the backbone of the army of the king of Jerusalem. They were all trained, fit warriors, and they were willing to undertake all the most dangerous duties in the Holy Land. If a castle lay in such an exposed position that no ordinary lord dare defend it, knights from one of the orders would be glad to hold it. Great sums of money were donated to the orders, and they soon became so rich and powerful that they were feared by Saracen and Christian alike.

The effigy of a Knight Templar in Temple Church, London.

6 THE SARACENS STRIKE BACK

The Second Crusade

One of the reasons for the First Crusade's success was that the Saracens were hopelessly divided. However, by the middle of the twelfth century, Muslims were more united. A powerful Muslim army captured the great city of Edessa, massacring all the Christians inside.

News of the disaster caused consternation in Europe. The pope decided that a new Crusade must be preached at once. Priests whipped up crusading zeal with frenzied speeches to large crowds, encouraging thousands to

volunteer for the holy mission.

In 1147, two ill-fated expeditions set out for the Holy Land. The German Emperor Conrad marched to Constantinople with a large force. But once in Asia Minor, disaster struck. His ill-disciplined troops were caught by the Turks near Dorylaeum. Although Conrad and his knights were able to fight their way out, most of his army was massacred or enslaved. Conrad sailed to Palestine with what was left.

King Louis VII of France fared little better. His troops were ambushed in the mountains of northern Syria. Thousands were killed and all his baggage was lost. The king himself barely escaped with his life. Only a fraction of his original force reached Palestine.

Once in the Holy Land, the two leaders, Louis and Conrad, joined forces with King Baldwin II of Jerusalem. But instead of trying to recapture Edessa, they attacked Damascus. The attack failed, and after many arguments the crusaders went home. The Second Crusade was a disaster. Two great armies had set out from Europe and after appalling losses had achieved nothing.

Left *In 1147 the crusaders, led by King Louis VII of France, were ambushed in the mountains of northern Syria.*

43

Above *After his victory at the battle of Hattin in 1187, Saladin found the remnants of the crusading army exhausted and unable to fight.*

A Persian drawing of Saladin, leader of the Saracens.

The great Saladin

The man who united all the Saracens in the east was the great Muslim leader, Saladin. Many of his soldiers were volunteers who came to fight the "Jihad," or Holy War, against the Christians — though like the crusaders they also had a healthy interest in plunder. By the 1180s they threatened the crusader states everywhere.

In the Christian camp things were not happy. King Guy of Jerusalem was a weak man, who was shown little respect by his nobles. However, in the summer of 1187 he gathered a large army and marched to attack Saladin.

It was an unusually hot summer. As the Christian army marched through Galilee, they found most of the wells dry. Horsemen from Saladin's army set fire to the hillsides and the crusaders found themselves marching through clouds of choking ash. By mid-afternoon on July 3, the Christian army was suffering severely from

heat and thirst. Though only three miles from Lake Tiberius and water, Guy ordered the army to halt at Hattin, acting on the advice of the Templar leader. The decision was fatal. The well at Hattin was dry.

At sunrise the next day, Saladin attacked. Driven crazy by thirst, the crusading army collapsed. Men flung away their weapons and fled for the lake. The king and his knights made a stand on a small hill, but the situation was hopeless. When Saladin made his final charge he found the surviving knights lying on the ground, overcome with heat and thirst.

All the crusading states now lay in Saladin's grasp. One castle after another fell to his army. The price of slaves fell so low that one Muslim soldier swapped a Christian for a pair of old shoes. On October 2, 1187, Saladin entered Jerusalem.

Above *Saladin was Richard the Lionheart's greatest rival.*

The Third Crusade

Below *Richard's archers helped the crusading army to defeat Saladin at the battle of Arsuf in 1191.*

Europe was stunned by the news of the Christian defeat at Hattin. The terrible news reached Richard the Lionheart as he besieged a small castle in the south of France.

All the great leaders of Europe vowed to avenge the loss of Jerusalem. The Emperor Barbarossa's great army disappeared in the graveyard of Asia Minor (see page 37). King Philip of France hated King Richard, and left the crusade as soon as Acre had fallen. This left Richard the Lionheart in sole command of the Third Crusade.

Richard was a very great military commander. In the past, crusading armies had relied almost entirely on their knights. Richard cleverly used his infantry to shield his knights' horses until the right moment came to charge. He also made greater use of his archers.

Once Acre had fallen, Richard marched south along the coast. He clashed with Saladin at the battle of Arsuf and won a resounding victory. But although he twice came within striking distance of Jerusalem, Richard realized that he would never capture the Holy City. Most of his crusaders wished to pray at the Holy Places and then go home. The Saracens *were* at home. The king knew it was time to make peace.

What Richard may not have fully realized was just how frightened Saladin was. If he had pressed a little harder he might have won back Jerusalem. But he would probably not have been able to hold it.

Richard's treaty with Saladin safeguarded the rights of unarmed pilgrims to visit the Holy Places in Jerusalem. He had proved that Christians could still defeat the Saracens. But as he set sail for England, the crusaders in the Holy Land must have despaired. Their lands were now reduced to a narrow strip along the coast.

Below *In this romantic painting, the artist portrays Richard the Lionheart and Saladin fighting. In fact, the two leaders never met face to face in battle.*

7 A HOPELESS CAUSE

Further Crusades

To many, the Crusades seemed hopeless, but expeditions still set out enthusiastically from Europe. The Fourth Crusade is one of the most notorious. It never reached the Holy Land at all. The crusaders sailed to Constantinople and plundered and burned the city instead.

In 1215, another Crusade was preached. The Fifth Crusade planned to attack Cairo in Egypt, as this was

Below *In 1229 the German emperor, Frederick II, signed a treaty with the Sultan Al-Kamil which gave Jerusalem back to the crusaders.*

considered to be the weak point in the Muslim Empire. For three years the crusaders floundered around in Egypt, but achieved very little.

The German Emperor, Frederick II, was one of the most complex men of his age. He conducted the Sixth Crusade by diplomacy rather than war. In 1229, he persuaded the Saracens to give up Jerusalem, but it was only a paper victory. The Muslims could recapture the city whenever they liked. They did so fifteen years later.

The popular and devout Louis IX of France was so pious that he was later made a saint. He led two expeditions. On the Seventh Crusade he again tried to attack the Saracens at their weak point in Cairo. But after successfully capturing the fortress of Damietta in 1250, his army became bogged down as the Nile River began to flood. Louis and most of his army were captured.

Twenty years later, Louis tried again. This time he landed in Tunisia, hoping to attack the Saracens from there. But a few months later he died, having failed to regain Jerusalem.

Above *This sixteenth century woodcut shows Louis IX (St. Louis) captured by the Saracens in 1250.*

Below *The fortress of Damietta in Egypt changed hands several times during the Crusades. Here it is being besieged by the crusaders in 1218 during the Fifth Crusade.*

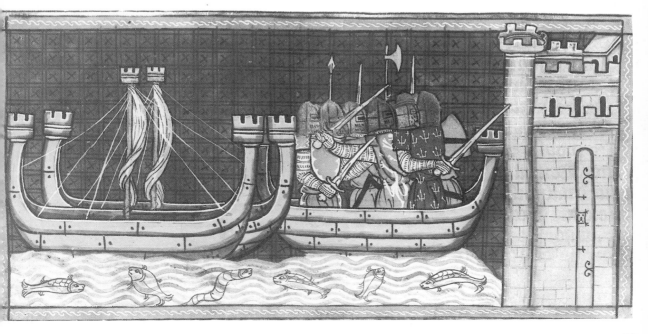

The Children's Crusade

The Children's Crusade was perhaps the most heart-rending expedition of them all. A twelve-year-old peasant boy, named Stephen of Cloyes, claimed Christ had appeared to him in a vision, and told him to organize a Crusade. Only innocent children, he declared, would be able to work the miracle that would free Jerusalem.

The King of France and his nobles refused to take the

boy seriously. But Pope Innocent III lent his support. "The very children put us to shame," he told the nobles. In the summer of 1212, thirty thousand girls and boys gathered behind their boy-preacher. They set off to walk to the Holy Land, hoping that God would look after them on the way, for they took no provisions.

Many starved before they had even marched through France. Arriving at the Mediterranean Sea, the children waited for the waters to divide before them, for this is the miracle that they had been told would happen. When the sea remained stubbornly in place, two crafty merchants named Hugh the Iron and William the Pig offered to take the children to Palestine by boat. Instead they sailed to North Africa, and sold the youthful crusaders in the Arab slave markets. It is said that only one survivor returned, after an imprisonment of eighteen years.

Twenty thousand children also set out enthusiastically from Germany. Hundreds died miserably as they marched south over the bleak mountain passes of the Alps. When the remainder reached southern Italy, the Bishop of Brindisi told them to go home. Very few survived the return journey. This tragic story is thought to have inspired the legend of the Pied Piper.

Above *The tragic Children's Crusade may have given rise to the story of the Pied Piper of Hamelin, whose music cleared the town of a plague of rats.*

Left *Stephen of Cloyes leads thousands of children on a hopeless Crusade. It never reached the Holy Land, and, it is said, only one child returned.*

51

8 COLLAPSE

The Saracen tide

Above *An Italian merchant wears the robes of the Order of the Knights of St. John.*

After 1270, the permanent settlers in the Holy Land had given up any thought of victory. The "barons of the land" were cooped up in their castles, ever fearful of another Saracen attack. In the great seaports, Italian merchants grew rich trading with the infidels, but still quarreled hopelessly among themselves, Venetians versus Genoese. Even the knights of the orders quarreled — Templars bickering with Hospitalers.

The end came swiftly. In 1289, Tripoli fell to the Saracens, and the town was completely destroyed. In 1291 it was Acre's turn. The citizens resisted desperately, the knights of the orders fighting to the death, but the Saracen tide was too strong. A few escaped to Cyprus; others were massacred or enslaved. The price of a western slave girl fell to less than a penny. The Muslims deliberately destroyed Acre, pulling down fortifications,

palaces and churches. In a few years that once great city was no more than a shabby village. By the end of the year there were no more crusaders left in the Holy Land.

That was the end of the Crusades, though the idea of freeing Jerusalem still haunted Europeans. Henry IV of England was pleased when a prophesy decreed he would die in the Holy City (in fact he died in the Jerusalem Chamber of the Palace of Westminster). Christopher Columbus hoped that the gold of the Americas would be used to free Jerusalem. Even that most down-to-earth king, Henry VII, toyed with the idea of leading a Crusade.

Of the knightly orders, the Templars were brutally suppressed in 1308. The Order of the Knights of St. John still exists and the St. John's Ambulance is still active in many parts of the world today.

Below *Men, women and children fled for their lives, as the Saracens fought their way into Acre despite heroic resistance by the knights of the orders.*

The legacy

The Crusades are an extraordinary episode in world history. For 200 years, west met east in a series of bloody encounters. Yet both sides, Muslim and Christian, learned from the other. If the crusaders probably gained more, it is because they had more to learn.

New goods were brought back to Europe in much greater numbers during the Crusades. Cotton appeared for the first time, as did cotton paper which soon replaced expensive parchment. A host of exotic foods and spices began to grace the tables of rich westerners — cloves, cinnamon, nutmeg, eastern fruits, and, most importantly, sugar. The knight also appreciated the comforts that he found in the east. Many a hardy crusader returned with tapestries and carpets to brighten his gloomy castle.

Arab learning slowly filtered back to Europe, particularly Arab discoveries in mathematics and medicine. As we have seen, military techniques also changed. The idea that battles should be fought by knights persisted right through the Middle Ages, but more intelligent commanders began to make better use of their footsoldiers and archers. Castle fortifications were also improved.

The knight himself also changed, though this has been exaggerated. By Richard I's time, poems and songs taught that a knight should behave more gently and fight only for good causes — not just for his own selfish ends. They were also encouraged to respect women and do good deeds to please her. This idea of "chivalry," which was so important in the Middle Ages, was partly inspired by the lofty ideals and dreams of the Crusades.

Opposite *The illustration shows a portrait of the two great rivals of the Third Crusade, Saladin and King Richard; a crusading knight; Caernarvon Castle, built in 1283 along the lines of castles the crusaders came across in Palestine; and a Muslim astronomer studying a meteor with a quadrant.*

Table of dates

325 The Emperor Constantine makes Christianity the official religion of the Roman Empire.

622 Mohammed begins preaching the religion of Islam.

638 Jerusalem occupied by the Arabs.

c1050 Seljuk Turks appear on the edge of the Byzantine Empire.

1071 The Emperor Romanus Diogenes defeated by the Turks at the Battle of Manzikert.

1095 Pope Urban II appeals for a Crusade to rescue the Holy Places.

1096 The People's Crusade.

1097 First Crusade gathers at Constantinople.
Battle of Dorylaeum (July 1).
Siege of Antioch begins (October).

1098 Antioch captured (June 5); besieging Saracens defeated (June 28).

1099 Jerusalem captured by the First Crusade (July 18).

1123 Order of the Knights Templar founded.

1144 Saracens capture the crusader state of Edessa.

1147 Start of the Second Crusade.

1148 Crusaders attack Damascus. Quarrels between leaders end the campaign.

1157 Birth of King Richard.

1169 Saladin unites Saracens under him.

1187 Saladin defeats Christian army at the battle of Hattin (July 4) and captures Jerusalem (October 2).

1189 Richard becomes king of England.

1190 Start of the Third Crusade.
The Emperor Barbarossa loses most of his army in Asia Minor and is himself drowned.

1191 Richard captures Cyprus (May), and arrives at Acre (June 8).
Acre falls to the Crusaders (12 July).
The king of France and the duke of Austria go home.
Richard defeats Saladin at the battle of Arsuf (September 7).

1192 Richard marches on Jerusalem and defeats Saladin at Jaffa.
Treaty concluded between Richard and Saladin (September 2).
Richard travels homeward, but is imprisoned by the duke of Austria.

1193 Death of Saladin.

1194 Richard returns to England after the payment of an enormous ransom.

1199 Richard dies from an arrow wound.

1204 Capture of Constantinople by the Fourth Crusade.

1212 The Children's Crusade.

1221 Fifth Crusade gives up after three years in Egypt.

1229 Frederick II of Germany negotiates the return of Jerusalem to the crusaders.

1244 Jerusalem retaken by the Saracens.
Crusaders defeated at the battle of La Forbie.

1248 Launch of the Seventh Crusade.

1250 Defeat of Seventh Crusade in Egypt and capture of St. Louis.

1270 Eighth Crusade attacks Tunisia. St. Louis dies on campaign.

1291 The fall of Acre, the last crusader fortress in the Holy Land.

1308 Order of the Knights Templar suppressed.

New words

Assassins A group of fanatical killers founded by the Persian Hasan as-Sabath. They were finally defeated by the Mongols in 1256.

Ballad A simple song, or a poem set to music.

Barbarian A savage, uncivilized and un-Christian tribesman.

Bazaar An eastern market.

Brigand A robber or a pirate.

Byzantine Term used to describe the eastern Roman Empire, centered in Constantinople (or Byzantium).

Caravan A group of merchants traveling together for safety in the east.

Carnage The bloody results of a slaughter or a massacre.

Chivalry Politeness and courtesy shown by knights toward women in the Middle Ages.

Chronicler A person who records historical events soon after they have happened.

Diplomacy The effort to solve problems between countries by talking about them without resorting to violence.

Falcon A bird of prey used in the popular medieval sport of falconry.

Famine Extreme scarcity of food, often leading to starvation.

Feudalism A system of ordering society in early medieval times when people promised loyalty and service in war in return for protection and the use of land belonging to the king or nobleman.

Hold The space below a ship's deck where cargo is stored.

Hospitalers An order of fighting monks founded in 1100. Their proper name was the Order of the Knights of St. John.

Hysteria An overexcited state of mind close to madness.

Infidel The term that Christians used for people who did not worship the Christian God.

Islam A religious faith held by Muslims.

Jihad The Islamic name for a "Holy War."

Lance A horseman's spear.

Motte and bailey castle A fortified mound of earth surrounded by a large wooden fence.

Myth A story that is not based on facts and so is unlikely to be true.

Nomad A wandering tribesman without a fixed home.

Peasant A member of the poorest class of people.

Pilgrim A person who makes a journey to a Holy Place for religious reasons.

Pillage/plunder To seize goods in war that do not belong to you.

Ransom A sum of money paid to the captors in return for the release of the captive.

Saracen A word used by crusaders to describe all Muslims in the Holy Land. It comes from the Arabic word "Sharkeyn," meaning eastern.

Scimitar A short, razor-sharp, curved sword used by the Saracens.

Steppes Vast, treeless plains stretching across central Russia.

Truce An agreement between two warring countries to stop fighting for a while.

Turban The Muslim headdress made up by coiling a length of cloth around the head.

Further information

Alladin, Bilzik. *The Story of Mohammed the Prophet.* Pomona, CA: Auromere, 1979.

Gibson, Michael and Pike, Trisha. *All About Knights.* St. Paul, MN: EMC, 1982.

Hayes, K.H.A. *Stories of Great Muslims.* Chicago: Kazi Publications, 1981.

Peach, L. Dugarde. *Richard the Lion Heart.* Bedford Hills, NY: Merry Thoughts, 1968.

Powell, Anton. *The Rise of Islam.* New York: Franklin Watts, 1980.

Treece, Henry. *Know About the Crusades.* Chester Springs, PA: Dufour, 1967.

Williams, Ann. *The Crusades.* New York: Longman, 1975.

Williams, Jay. *Knights of the Crusades.* New York: Harper & Row, 1962.

INDEX

Picture acknowledgments

The illustrations in this book were supplied by: BBC Hulton Picture Library 5, 24, 41; Mansell Collection 9 (below), 15, 16, 19, 21, 27, 29, 31 (top), 44, 49, (both), 51, 52; Mary Evans Picture Library 45. The remainder are from the Wayland Picture Library.